# HOW SMART ARE YOU?

# TEST YOUR BASEBALL IQ

Dean Mathewson

BLACK DOG & LEVENTHAL PUBLISHERS
NEW YORK

Copyright © 1994 by Black Dog & Leventhal Publishers Inc.

All rights reserved. No part of this book may be reproduced in any form or by any electronic or mechanical means including information storage and retrieval systems without written permission of the publisher.

Published by

**Black Dog & Leventhal Publishers Inc.**
151 West 19th Street
New York, New York 10011

Distributed by

**Workman Publishing Company**
708 Broadway
New York, New York 10003

**ISBN: 0-9637056-5-2**

# CONTENTS

| | |
|---|---|
| *Dabbler* Questions | 5 |
| *Dabbler* Answers | 19 |
| | |
| *Smarter-than-Most* Questions | 25 |
| *Smarter-than-Most* Answers | 39 |
| | |
| *Genius* Questions | 43 |
| *Genius* Answers | 59 |

# Introduction

How smart are you? We can't answer that question for you generally, but this book certainly can determine your standing among the heavy-hitters in baseball knowledge.

After taking the quizzes spanning Dabbler, Smarter-Than-Most, and Genius levels, calculating exactly what kind of masterful grasp of baseball you have will be the easy part.

Each level has sixty-six or sixty-seven questions totaling two hundred questions in all. To get a true reading on your ability, take the tests adhering to the allotted time limits stated at the beginning of each section. Almost all the questions are multiple choice. There are no tricks, just compelling, fascinating, and strange baseball trivia.

Once you complete the test, check the answer key at the end of that section and tally up your scores. Now you are equipped with all the information you need to spin the wheel and verify in seconds where your level of mastery lies.

All you have to do is turn to the front cover, and line up the number you answered correctly in the window on the scoring wheel. There are windows for each test level, so you can see how you fared with the Dabbler, Smarter-Than-Most, and genius questions, as well as cumulatively.

# *Dabbler* Questions

*Time limit: 60 minutes*

1. **Take a Number! Match the player with his jersey number:**

   1. Reggie Jackson      a. 41
   2. Ernie Banks         b. 1
   3. Tom Seaver          c. 8
   4. Babe Ruth           d. 44
   5. Yogi Berra          e. 3

2. **Who holds the record for the most seasons played on the same team?**
   a. George Brett (Kansas City Royals)
   b. Stan Musial (St. Louis Cardinals)
   c. Brooks Robinson (Baltimore Orioles)
   d. Lou Gehrig (New York Yankees)
   e. Ernie Banks (Chicago Cubs)

3. **Rank each player according to their highest number of home runs in a season:**
   a. Hank Aaron
   b. Willie Mays
   c. Jimmie Foxx
   d. Roger Maris
   e. Babe Ruth

4. **Who is the only pitcher to hold back to back no hitters?**
   a. Allie Reynolds
   b. Jim Maloney
   c. Johnny Vander Meer
   d. Sandy Koufax
   e. Nolan Ryan

## 5  Match the announcer with the team:

1. Mel Allen
2. Vin Scully
3. Skip Caray
4. Harry Caray
5. Ralph Kiner

a. Braves
b. Cubs
c. Mets
d. Yankees
e. Dodgers

## 6  Who holds the National League record for the most home runs in a single season?

a. Mike Schmidt
b. Mel Ott
c. Ralph Kiner
d. Willie Stargell
e. Hack Wilson

## 7  Who holds the record for the most career home runs in the world series?

a. Reggie Jackson
b. Mickey Mantle
c. Yogi Berra
d. Don Baylor
e. Duke Snider

## 8  Rank in chronological order:

a. Last player to hit over 50 HRs in a season
b. The designated hitter is adopted by the American League
c. Last player to win the triple crown
d. First players' strike
e. First world series game to be played at night

## 9  Match the owner with the team.

1. Gene Autry
2. George Steinbrenner
3. Marge Schott
4. Walter O'Malley
5. Charlie Finley

a. New York Yankees
b. California Angels
c. Los Angeles Dodgers
d. Cincinatti Reds
e. Oakland Athletics

## 10 Match the player with his claim to fame:

1. Tracy Stallard
2. Vic Wertz
3. Eric Show
4. Dale Mitchell
5. Ralph Branca

a. Gave up Bobby Thomson's home run in the 1951 Playoffs
b. Surrendered Pete Rose's 4,192nd hit
c. Last batter out in Don Larsen's perfect game
d. Gave up Roger Maris' 61st home run
e. Was at bat when Willie Mays made his famous catch in the 1954 World Series

## 11 What team holds the record for the longest consecutive winning streak?

a. 1984 Detroit Tigers
b. 1935 Chicago Cubs
c. 1951 New York Giants
d. 1916 New York Giants
e. 1906 Chicago White Sox

## 12 Who recorded the lowest single-season ERA since 1900 (250 or more innings)?

a. Ed Walsh
b. "Three-Finger" Mordecai Brown
c. Ed Reulbach
d. Addie Joss
e. Bob Gibson

## 13 Who holds the record for the most home runs by a rookie?

a. Jimmy Wynn
b. Daryl Strawberry
c. Barry Bonds
d. Mark McGwire
e. José Canseco

## 14 Match the person with the quote:

1. Ernie Banks
2. Yogi Berra
3. Leo Durocher
4. Lou Gehrig
5. Roy Campanella

a. "Nice guys finish last."
b. "You gotta be a man to play baseball for a living but you gotta have a lot of boy in you too."
c. "I count myself the luckiest man on the face of the earth."
d. "What a great day for baseball. Let's play two."
e. "It ain't over till it's over."

## 15 Who holds the record for the most consecutive games hitting a home run?

a. Ted Kluszewski
b. Dale Long
c. Dave Kingman
d. Dave Mattingly
e. Greg Luzinski

## 16 Who holds the record for the most times hitting a home run as a lefty and a righty in the same game?

a. Ken Henderson
b. Reggie Smith
c. Eddie Murray
d. Pete Rose
e. Mickey Mantle

## 17 Since 1900 what pitcher has won the most games in a single season?

a. Jack Chesbro
b. "Iron Joe" McGinnity
c. Denny McLain
d. Addie Joss
e. Bill Dinneen

## 18 What pitcher struck out the most batters in one game?

   a. Tom Seaver
   b. Ron Guidry
   c. Roger Clemens
   d. Ramon Martinez
   e. Steve Carlton

## 19 Who was the first player to earn $100,000 in a season?

   a. Joe DiMaggio
   b. Babe Ruth
   c. Ted Williams
   d. Dizzy Dean
   e. Frankie Frisch

## 20 Life after baseball. Match the player with endorsement:

   1. Phil Rizzuto
   2. Joe Dimaggio
   3. Jim Palmer
   4. Bob Uecker
   5. Yogi Berra

   a. Jockey Underwear
   b. Yoo-Hoo Chocolate Drink
   c. Miller Lite
   d. Mr. Coffee
   e. The Money Store

## 21 What left-handed pitcher has the most career victories?

   a. Lefty Grove
   b. Walter Johnson
   c. Warren Spahn
   d. Steve Carlton
   e. Eddie Plank

## 22 What player has the highest career on-base percentage?

   a. Wade Boggs
   b. Ted Williams
   c. Rogers Hornsby
   d. Babe Ruth
   e. Joe Jackson

## 23 Who has the most base hits in world series play?

   a. Yogi Berra
   b. Joe Morgan
   c. Mickey Mantle
   d. Babe Ruth
   e. Pee Wee Reese

## 24 Who has collected the most hits in All-Star game play?

   a. Stan Musial
   b. Pete Rose
   c. Dave Winfield
   d. Willie Mays
   e. George Brett

## 25 Match the team with its nickname:

   1. New York Yankees      a. The Whiz Kids
   2. St. Louis Cardinals   b. The Amazin's
   3. Cincinnati Reds       c. Murderer's Row
   4. Philadelphia Phillies d. The Gas House Gang
   5. New York Mets         e. The Big Machine

## 26 Which brothers combined for the most victories in one season?

   a. Jim and Gaylord Perry
   b. Christy and Henry Mathewson
   c. Phil and Joe Niekro
   d. Harry and Stan Coveleski
   e. Paul and Dizzy Dean

## 27 What team holds the record for the most home runs in a season?

a. 1987 Chicago Cubs
b. 1927 New York Yankees
c. 1961 New York Yankees
d. 1956 Cincinatti Reds
e. 1947 New York Giants

## 28 Match the minor league team with its parent club:

1. New York Mets
2. L. A. Dodgers
3. San Diego Padres
4. St. Louis Cardinals
5. Boston Red Sox

a. Louisville
b. Pawtucket
c. Tidewater
d. Albuquerque
e. Las Vegas

## 29 Who is the only player to bat over .400 in two consecutive world series?

a. Thurman Munson
b. Johnny Bench
c. Bobby Richardson
d. Lou Brock
e. Rickey Henderson

## 30 Who holds record for the most base hits in a single season?

a. Rod Carew
b. Rogers Hornsby
c. Wade Boggs
d. George Sisler
e. Nap Lajoie

## 31 Who holds the National League record, since 1900, for the most consecutive seasons batting over .300?

a. Pete Rose
b. Honus Wagner
c. Tony Gwyn
d. Stan Musial
e. Rogers Hornsby

<u>Baseball Dabbler Questions</u>

## 32 What batter holds the lifetime record for most times hit by a pitch?

   a. Ron Santo
   b. Don Baylor
   c. Ron Hunt
   d. Ken Henderson
   e. Dwight Evans

## 33 What is the only 2B-SS combination to play regularly for the same team for over 10 years?

   a. Davey Lopes and Bill Russell
   b. Lou Whittaker and Alan Trammel
   c. Nellie Fox and Luis Aparicio
   d. Frank White and Freddie Patek
   e. Bill Mazeroski and Dick Groat

## 34 Who is the only shortstop to hit 30 home runs, drive in 100 or more runs and hit over .300 ?

   a. Cal Ripken Jr.
   b. Ernie Banks
   c. Lou Boudreau
   d. Luke Appling
   e. Toby Harrah

## 35 What pitcher has the highest winning percentage (minimum 15 wins)?

   a. Ron Guidry
   b. Rick Sutcliffe
   c. Roy Face
   d. Sal Malgie
   e. Preacher Roe

## 36 What pitcher lost the most games during his career?

   a. Bobo Newsome
   b. Phil Niekro
   c. Cy Young
   d. Early Wynn
   e. Robin Roberts

## 37 Who has the most combined HR's and stolen bases in a season (minimum 30 home runs)?

   a. Eric Davis
   b. Howard Johnson
   c. Barry Bonds
   d. José Canseco
   e. Rickey Henderson

## 38 What player had the most 30-30 seasons (HR & SB)?

   a. Eric Davis
   b. Bobby Bonds
   c. Daryl Strawberry
   d. Willie Mays
   e. Mickey Mantle

## 39 What pitcher holds the record for the most strikeouts in a world series game?

   a. Moe Drabowsky
   b. Don Drysdale
   c. Sandy Koufax
   d. Bob Gibson
   e. Don Larsen

## 40 What team's starting four pitchers combined for the most victories?

   a. 1965 Los Angeles Dodgers
   b. 1904 New York Giants
   c. 1910 Philadelphia Atheletics
   d. 1927 New York Yankees
   e. 1971 Baltimore Orioles

## 41 Who holds the major league record for most RBI's in a season?

a. Hack Wilson
b. Hank Greenberg
c. Lou Gerhig
d. Jimmie Foxx
e. Stan Musial

## 42 Who holds the National League record for the longest hitting streak since 1900?

a. Tony Gwynn
b. Bill Madlock
c. Pete Rose
d. Stan Musial
e. Steve Garvey

## 43 Who holds the record for most consecutive stolen bases without being caught?

a. Willie Wilson
b. Vince Coleman
c. Tim Raines
d. Maury Wills
e. Davey Lopes

## 44 Whose record for all-time hits did Pete Rose break?

a. Stan Musial
b. Wee Wee Keller
c. Ty Cobb
d. Hank Aaron
e. Honus Wagner

## 45 He had to wait to be immortalized. Who doesn't belong?

a. Cy Young
b. Babe Ruth
c. Honus Wagner
d. Christy Mathewson
e. Ty Cobb

## 46 Who is the youngest player to ever win back-to-back MVP awards?

  a. Jimmie Foxx
  b. Ernie Banks
  c. Dale Murphy
  d. Joe Morgan
  e. Mickey Mantle

## 47 What pitcher has won the most Cy Young awards?

  a. Sandy Koufax
  b. Roger Clemens
  c. Steve Carlton
  d. Jim Palmer
  e. Bob Gibson

## 48 Who is the only player to win the MVP in both leagues?

  a. Kirk Gibson
  b. Frank Robinson
  c. Ken Singleton
  d. Frank Howard
  e. Billy Williams

## 49 Which stadium doesn't belong?

  a. Shea Stadium
  b. Veteran's Stadium
  c. Three Rivers Stadium
  d. Olympic Stadium
  e. Busch Stadium

## 50 Match the team with its former stadium:

  a. Brooklyn Dodgers
  b. Cincinatti Reds
  c. Pittsburgh Pirates
  d. Baltimore Orioles
  e. Philadelphia Athletics

  1. Memorial Stadium
  2. Forbes Field
  3. Crosley Field
  4. Shibe Park
  5. Ebbets Field

## 51 Match the current team name with its former name:

| | | | |
|---|---|---|---|
| a. | Twins | 1. | Browns |
| b. | Yankees | 2. | Colt 45's |
| c. | Orioles | 3. | Pilots |
| d. | Brewers | 4. | Highlanders |
| e. | Astros | 5. | Senators |

## 52 Rank the following players from most career stolen bases to the least:

a. Ty Cobb
b. Lou Brock
c. Tim Raines
d. Rickey Henderson
e. Joe Morgan

## 53 Who is only rookie to win the ERA crown?

a. Dwight Gooden
b. Tom Seaver
c. Hoyt Wilhelm
d. Jim Bunning
e. Dean Chance

## 54 Who is the youngest pitcher to pitch in a major league game?

a. Bob Feller
b. Von McDaniel
c. Gary Nolan
d. Joe Nuxhall
e. Jim Derrington

## 55 Who was the youngest regular to play in the majors?

a. Johnny Bench
b. Robin Yount
c. Mel Ott
d. Mickey Mantle
e. Ron LeFlore

## 56 What rookie holds the record for the longest hitting streak?

a. Manny Sanguillen
b. Lou Pinella
c. Benito Santiago
d. Jim Eisenreich
e. Jimmy Piersall

## 57 What shortstop holds the record for the most consecutive chances without an error?

a. Cal Ripken
b. Ozzie Smith
c. Mark Belanger
d. Rabbit Maranville
e. Phil Rizzuto

## 58 Who holds the record for the most saves in a season?

a. Dave Righetti
b. Dennis Eckersley
c. Lee Smith
d. Willie Hernandez
e. Bobby Thigpen

## 59 Who recorded the only no-hit win on an opening day?

a. Fernando Valenzuela
b. Bob Feller
c. Bob Lemon
d. Allie Reynolds
e. Len Barker

## 60 What pitcher has had the most opening day assignments?

a. Whitey Ford
b. Tom Seaver
c. Jim Palmer
d. Warren Spahn
e. Robin Roberts

## 61 "Over There." Who doesn't fit?

a. Ted Williams
b. Willie Mays
c. Duke Snider
d. Stan Musial
e. Joe DiMaggio

## 62 What manager led his team to a record five consecutive world series victories?

a. Joe McCarthy
b. John McGraw
c. Ralph Houk
d. Casey Stengel
e. Connie Mack

## 63 Who was the first African-American pitcher in the major leagues?

a. Don Newcombe
b. Dan Bankhead
c. Joe Black
d. Satchel Paige
e. Sam Jones

## 64 What manager has won the most league championships?

a. Tony Larussa
b. Earl Weaver
c. Sparky Anderson
d. Tommy Lasorda
e. Jim Leyland

## 65 Who holds the record for the most strike-outs in a single season?

a. José Canseco
b. Dave Kingman
c. Bobby Bonds
d. Gorman Thomas
e. Dick Allen

## 66 Match the player with the feat:

1. Joe Jackson
2. Al Kaline
3. Carl Furillo
4. Ty Cobb
5. Carl Yastrzemski

a. He was the youngest player to win the batting crown.
b. He won the most consecutive batting titles.
c. He had the highest batting average without winning the batting crown.
d. This league leader in batting had the biggest leap in average from the previous season.
e. He had the lowest batting average that captured the league batting crown.

# Dabbler Answers

*(Score 1 point for each correct answer. For multiple choice score 1 point if all are correct; 1/2 point if 3 are correct.)*

1. 1-d, 2-b, 3-a, 4-e, 5-c
2. c. Brooks Robinson played 23 years for the Baltimore Orioles.
3. d (Roger Maris, 61 in 1961), e (Babe Ruth, 60 in 1927), c (Jimmie Foxx, 58 in 1932), b (Willie Mays, 52 in 1965), a (Hank Aaron, 47 in 1971)
4. c. Johnny Vander Meer no-hit the Boston Braves on June 11, 1938 and then in his next start repeated the feat by no-hitting the Brooklyn Dodgers.
5. 1-d, 2-e, 3-a, 4-b, 5-c
6. e. Chicago Cub Hack Wilson hit 56 home runs in the 1930 season.
7. b. Mickey Mantle hit 18 home runs in 12 world series appearances.

<u>Baseball Dabbler Answers</u>

8. c (1967), e (1971), d (1972), b (1973), a (1991)
9. 1-b, 2-a, 3-d, 4-c, 5-e
10. 1-d, 2-e, 3-b, 4-c, 5-a
11. d. The 1916 New York Giants were winners in twenty-six straight games.
12. e. In 1968 Bob Gibson had a 1.12 ERA. The following year a rule change was made to make the strike zone smaller.
13. 1-d, 2-e, 3-a, 4-c, 5-b
14. d. Mark McGwire hit 49 home runs in his 1987 rookie season for the Oakland A's.
15. b & d. Both Mattingly and Long went 8 consecutive games with a home run.
16. e. Mickey Mantle did it 10 times in his 18-year career.
17. a. New York Yankee pitcher Jack Chesbro won 41 games in 1904.
18. c. Roger Clemens struck out 20 Seattle Mariners in one game during the 1986 season.
19. a. Joe DiMaggio received a $100,000 salary in the 1949 season.
20. 1-e, 2-d, 3-a, 4-c, 5-b
21. c. Warren Spahn won 363 games to lead all lefties.
22. b. Ted Williams has a .483 lifetime OBP
23. a. Yogi Berra had 71 in 14 world series appearances.
24. d. Willie Mays has 23 hits in the all-star game.
25. 1-c, 2-d, 3-e, 4-a, 5-b
26. e. In 1934 Paul and Dizzy Dean combined for 49 victories while pitching for the St. Louis Cardinals.
27. c. Led by Roger Maris' record setting 61 homers and Mantle's 54, the 1961 New York Yankees hit 240 home runs.
28. 1-c, 2-d, 3-e, 4-a, 5-b
29. d. St. Louis Cardinal outfielder Lou Brock hit .414 in the 1967 series and then went on to bat .464 against the Detroit Tigers in the 1968 fall classic.
30. d. George Sisler had 257 hits in 1920 for the St. Louis Browns.

31. d. Stan Musial hit over .300 in 16 consecutive seasons (1942-1958).
32. c. Ron Hunt was hit by a pitch a record setting 243 times during his 12-year major league career.
33. b. Lou Whittaker & Alan Trammel played regularly for the Detroit Tigers from 1978-1991. (Injuries forced Trammel to play only 29 games during the 1992 season.)
34. a. In 1991 Cal Ripken hit 34 home runs, drove in 114 runs and batted .323 en route to winning the American League MVP for the Baltimore Orioles.
35. c. Roy Face had a .947 winning percentage in 1959 (18-1).
36. c. Cy Young lost 316 games during his 22 year career.
37. a. In 1987, Cincinnatti Red Eric Davis hit 37 home runs and stole 50 bases for a record setting combined HR-SB total of 87.
38. b. Bobby Bonds did it 5 times (1969, 1973, 1975, 1977 & 1978).
39. d. Bob Gibson struck out 17 Detroit Tigers in the opening game of the 1968 World Series.
40. b. The 1904 New York Giants' starting 4, Joe McGinnity (35 wins), Christy Mathewson (31 wins), Dummy Taylor (21 wins) and Hooks Wiltse (13 wins), set a record with 110 wins by a starting  quartet.
41. a. In 1930, Hack Wilson drove in 190 runs for the Chicago Cubs.
42. c. Pete Rose hit in 44 consecutive games during the 1978 season.
43. b. Over the 1988 and 1989 seasons, St. Louis Cardinal Vince Coleman stole 50 bases before being caught.
44  c. With his 4,192 base hit, Pete Rose broke Ty Cobb's record.
45. a. Cy Young was the only player not elected to the Hall of Fame when it first opened.

Baseball Dabbler Answers

46. c. Dale Murphy was 27 years old when he won his second consecutive MVP award in 1983.
47. c. Steve Carlton has won the award 4 times (1972, 1977, 1980, 1982).
48. b. Frank Robinson won the National League MVP in 1961 as a Cincinatti Red and then was chosen as the American League MVP in 1966 while playing for the Baltimore Orioles.
49. a. Shea is the only stadium with a natural surface instead of astroturf.
50. 1-e, 2-c, 3-b, 4-a, 5-d
51. 1-e, 2-d, 3-a, 4-c, 5-b
52. d, b, a, c, e
53. c. New York Giant hurler Hoyt Wilhelm, in his rookie season of 1952, led all National League pitchers with an ERA of 2.43.
54. d. Joe Nuxhall at age 15 and 10 1/2 months pitched 2/3 of an inning for the Cincinnatti Reds in 1944. The Reds lost the game 18-0.
55. b. Robin Yount was 18 years old when he became the regular shortstop for the Milwaukee Brewers during the 1974 season.
56. c. Benito Santiago, San Diego catcher, hit in 34 consecutive games as a rookie in 1987.
57. a. In 1990 Cal Ripken fielded 431 chances without an error.
58. e. Bobby Thigpen, White Sox reliever, recorded a record setting 57 saves in the 1990 season.
59. c. Bob Feller no-hit the Chicago White Sox opening day 1940 to lead the Cleveland Indians to victory.
60. b. Tom Seaver has pitched 16 opening day games (13 in the NL and 3 in the AL).
61. c. Duke Snider is the only player whose career was not interrupted by military service.
62. d. Casey Stengel's New York Yankees were the world champion from 1949-1953.
63. b. Dan Bankhead was a relief pitcher for the Brooklyn Dodgers in 1947.

64. c. Sparky Anderson has guided his team to victory 5 times in league championship play. (4 times with Cincinnatti and once with Detroit).
65. c. Bobby Bonds set a record by striking out 189 times in 1970.
66. 1-c, 2-a, 3-d, 4-b, 5-e

# *Smarter-Than-Most* Questions

*(Time limit: 60 minutes)*

1 **Who has hit the most home runs in opening day games?**
   a. Lou Gehrig
   b. Stan Musial
   c. George Brett
   d. Frank Robinson
   e. Willie Stargell

2 **Who is the only batter to win a batting title in three different decades?**
   a. Pete Rose
   b. George Brett
   c. Carl Yastrzemski
   d. Rod Carew
   e. Billy Williams

3 **Since 1900, who is the only player to have led both leagues in home runs?**
   a. Dave Kingman
   b. Frank Robinson
   c. Bobby Murcer
   d. Sam Crawford
   e. Johnny Mize

4 **Who holds the all-time record for the most career grand slam home runs?**
   a. Harmon Killebrew
   b. Lou Gehrig
   c. Jimmie Foxx
   d. Reggie Jackson
   e. Don Mattingly

Baseball Smarter-Than-Most Questions

## 5 Which of these actors did not portray the following players on the screen?

a. William Bendix as Babe Ruth
b. Gary Cooper as Lou Gehrig
c. Anthony Perkins as Jimmy Piersall
d. Ronald Reagan as Walter Johnson
e. John Goodman as Babe Ruth

## 6 Match the Negro league team and its city:

1. Monarchs         a. Cincinnati-Indianapolis
2. Crawfords        b. Pittsburgh
3. Black Barons     c. Newark
4. Eagles           d. Kansas City
5. Clowns           e. Birmingham

## 7 What left-handed pitcher has struck out the most batters in his career?

a. Steve Carlton
b. Sandy Koufax
c. Lefty Grove
d. Warren Spahn
e. Carl Hubbell

## 8 What team has lost the most World Series?

a. New York Yankees
b. New York/San Francisco Giants
c. Pittsburgh Pirates
d. St. Louis Cardinals
e. Brooklyn/Los Angeles Dodgers

## 9 Match the team with the last year they won a World Series:

1. Chicago Cubs              a. 1957
2. Chicago White Sox         b. 1948
3. Cleveland Indians         c. 1918
4. Boston Red Sox            d. 1908
5. Milwaukee/Atlanta         e. 1917
   Braves

10 What 300 game winner had the fewest wins at age 30?

   a. Early Wynn
   b. Ferguson Jenkins
   c. Phil Niekro
   d. Nolan Ryan
   e. Gaylord Perry

11 What father-son combination has hit the most home runs?

   a. Gus and Buddy Bell
   b. Ken (Sr) and Ken (Jr) Griffey
   c. Roy (Sr) and Roy (Jr) Smalley
   d. Bobby and Barry Bonds
   e. Yogi and Dale Berra

12 Who has recorded 200 or more hits in the most consecutive seasons?

   a. Ty Cobb
   b. Rod Carew
   c. Stan Musial
   d. Wade Boggs
   e. Pete Rose

13 What player hit the most home runs in the 1950's?

   a. Willie Mays
   b. Mickey Mantle
   c. Duke Snider
   d. Ted Williams
   e. Eddie Mathews

14 Who pitched the most career shutouts?

   a. Walter Johnson
   b. Nolan Ryan
   c. Bob Gibson
   d. Christy Mathewson
   e. Lefty Grove

**Baseball Smarter-Than-Most Questions**

## 15 Who threw the most shutouts in one season?

   a. Mordecai Brown
   b. Don Drysdale
   c. Bob Gibson
   d. Grover Alexander
   e. Ed Walsh

## 16 What major league pitcher holds the record for the most consecutive victories in a single season?

   a. Richard "Rube" Marquard
   b. George Earnshaw
   c. Carl Hubbel
   d. Anthony Young
   e. Ed Reulbach

## 17 Who holds the record for the most consecutive seasons with 30 or more home runs?

   a. Mike Schmidt
   b. Ralph Kiner
   c. Hank Aaron
   d. Mel Ott
   e. Jimmie Foxx

## 18 Who holds the record for the most career pinch hit home runs?

   a. Cliff Johnson
   b. Manny Mota
   c. Smoky Burgess
   d. Vic Wertz
   e. Rusty Staub

## 19 Innocent until proven guilty. Who does not belong?

a. Pete Rose
b. Wille Mays
c. Ty Cobb
d. Mickey Mantle
e. Joe Jackson

## 20 Match the player with the scandal:

| | | |
|---|---|---|
| 1. Fritz Peterson | a. | Pitched a no-hitter while under the influence of LSD |
| 2. Pete Rose | b. | Suspended from baseball for cocaine abuse |
| 3. Steve Garvey | c. | Wife-swapping |
| 4. Dock Ellis | d. | Fathered illegitimate children |
| 5. Steve Howe | e. | Gambling |

## 21 What manager has the lowest lifetime winning percentage (min. 1,000 games)?

a. Gene Mauch
b. Burt Shotton
c. Dave Bristol
d. Fred Haney
e. Jimmie Wilson

## 22 What manager gave the following advice on handling a ball club?

"The secret to managing a club is keeping the five guys who hate you away from the five guys who haven't made up their minds."

a. Leo Durocher
b. Casey Stengel
c. Yogi Berra
d. John McGraw
e. Earl Weaver

## 23 Who was the first woman to run a major league baseball team?

- a. Joan Payson
- b. Marge Schott
- c. Helen Douglas
- d. Helen Britton
- e. Jeanette Rankin

## 24 Which player has had the most games with two or more home runs?

- a. Ralph Kiner
- b. Jimmie Foxx
- c. Babe Ruth
- d. Willie Mays
- e. Reggie Jackson

## 25 Who holds the record for the most consecutive games with an extra-base hit?

- a. Rogers Hornsby
- b. Paul Waner
- c. Freddy Lindstrom
- d. Chick Hafey
- e. Hack Wilson

## 26 What pitcher holds the record for the highest percentage of his team's wins in a season?

- a. Walter Johnson for the Washington Senators
- b. Warren Spahn for the Milwaukee Braves
- c. Phil Niekro for the Atlanta Braves
- d. Steve Carlton for the Philadelphia Phillies
- e. Robin Roberts for the Philadelphia Phillies

## 27 What pitcher won the most games in his first five full seasons in the major leagues?

- a. Roger Clemens
- b. Christy Mathewson
- c. Dwight Gooden
- d. Addie Joss
- e. Bob Feller

## 28 What pitcher holds the record for wins in a rookie season?

a. Lefty Grove
b. Grover "Pete" Alexander
c. Eddie Plank
d. Hippo Vaughn
e. Christy Mathewson

## 29 Who holds the record for the most consecutive games at catcher?

a. Bill Dickey
b. Wes Westrum
c. Frankie Hayes
d. Buddy Rosar
e. Jerry Grote

## 30 Who holds the record for the most career steals of home?

a. Eddie Collins
b. Rod Carew
c. Jackie Robinson
d. Ty Cobb
e. Frankie Frisch

## 31 Who holds the record for the most stolen bases in a game?

a. Vince Coleman
b. Ty Cobb
c. Lou Brock
d. Eddie Collins
e. Luis Aparicio

## 32 What team has lost the most consecutive games at the beginning of a season?

a. 1962 New York Mets
b. 1988 Atlanta Braves
c. 1961 Philadelphia Phillies
d. 1988 Baltimore Orioles
e. 1951 St. Louis Browns

## 33 What team had the worst record the year they won the world championship?

- a. 1969 New York Mets
- b. 1990 Cincinatti Reds
- c. 1987 Minnesota Twins
- d. 1959 Los Angeles Dodgers
- e. 1948 Boston Braves

## 34 What team has the worst winning percentage in a season?

- a. 1939 St. Louis Browns
- b. 1962 New York Mets
- c. 1935 Boston Braves
- d. 1916 Philadelphia Athletics
- e. 1942 Philadelphia Phillies

## 35 Who was the first Hispanic player inducted into the Hall of Fame?

- a. Luis Aparicio
- b. Roberto Clemente
- c. Juan Marichal
- d. Tony Oliva
- e. Matty Alou

## 36 Who is the only member of both the Baseball and Footballs Hall of Fame?

- a. Jim Thorpe
- b. George Halas
- c. Hank Soar
- d. Cal Hubbard
- e. Frankie Frisch

## 37 Who's the odd one out?

- a. Ernie Banks
- b. Ralph Kiner
- c. Gaylord Perry
- d. Ferguson Jenkins
- e. Reggie Jackson

### 38 Who was the only catcher to lead the National League in triples?

- a. Benito Santiago
- b. Tim McCarver
- c. Manny Sanguillen
- d. John Stearns
- e. Biff Pocoroba

### 39 Who has the most at-bats in a season without a stolen base?

- a. Don Mattingly
- b. Joe Torne
- c. Pete Rose
- d. Ted Williams
- e. Ted Kluszewski

### 40 Which pitcher gave up Hank Aaron's 715th homerun?

- a. Don Gullet
- b. Don Sutton
- c. Al Downing
- d. Jerry Koosman
- e. Ken Brett

### 41 Who allowed the most home runs in a single season?

- a. Anthony Young
- b. Dennis Leonard
- c. Bert Blyleven
- d. Floyd Bannister
- e. Jack Morris

### 42 What pitcher gave up the most home runs in his career?

- a. Jim Kaat
- b. Robin Roberts
- c. Warren Spahn
- d. Gaylord Perry
- e. Steve Carlton

## 43 Who was the last player to make an unassisted triple play?

- a. Ozzie Smith
- b. Mickey Morandiwi
- c. Doug Flynn
- d. Jimmy Woney
- e. Ron Hansen

## 44 Versatility. Who doesn't fit?

- a. Don Buford
- b. Lee Mazzilli
- c. Garry Templeton
- d. Paul Molitor
- e. Mickey Mantle

## 45 What pitcher has the most world series victories without a loss?

- a. Lefty Gomez
- b. Carl Mays
- c. Red Ruffing
- d. Jim Lonborg
- e. Don Gullet

## 46 Who is oldest pitcher to start a World Series game?

- a. Tommy John
- b. Carl Erskine
- c. Jack Quinn
- d. Howard Emtike
- e. George Earnshaw

## 47 Which came first? Rank each event from which occured first to most recent:

- a. First Black Major League umpire
- b. First Black Major League manager
- c. First Black rookie of the year
- d. First female umpire in professional baseball
- e. First non-white to be a New York Yankee

## 48 What pitcher holds the record for the most consecutive scoreless innings in world series play?

- a. Christy Mathewson
- b. Don Newcombe
- c. Whitey Ford
- d. Mickey Lolich
- e. Johnny Podres

## 49 Match the teenage player with the feat:

| | | |
|---|---|---|
| 1. Tony Conigliario | a. Most HRs in a season |
| 2. Phil Cavaretta | b. Most walks in a season |
| 3. Mel Ott | c. Most hits in a season |
| 4. Ty Cobb | d. Highest batting average in a season |
| 5. Rusty Staub | e. Most stolen bases in a season |

## 50 Match the teenage player with the feat:

1. Dwight Gooden — a. Most complete games by a pitcher in a season
2. Joe Wood — b. Most shutouts by a pitcher in a season
3. Wally Bunker — c. Lowest ERA
4. Bob Feller — d. Most strikeouts
5. Gary Nolan — e. Most wins

## 51 Match the player with the feat:

1. Tris Speaker — a. Most consecutive games with three or more hits
2. Ted Williams — b. Most consectves games with a base hit
3. George Brett — c. Most consecutive at bats with a base hit (bb not included)
4. Walt Dropo — d. Most consecutive at bats reaching base
5. Joe DiMaggio — e. Most hitting streaks over 20 games in his career

Baseball Smarter-Than-Most Questions

**52** Match the player with the player he replaced:

1. Doug DeCinces
2. Babe Dahlgren
3. Joe Pepitone
4. Carl Yastrzemski
5. Gary Maddox

a. Lou Gehrig
b. Mickey Mantle
c. Willie Mays
d. Ted Williams
e. Brooks Robinson

**53** What pitcher has recorded the most wins in League Championship play?

a. Steve Carlton
b. Mike Torrez
c. Jim Gullet
d. Jim Palmer
e. Dave Stewart

**54** What player was on deck when Bobby Thomson hit his home run that clinched the pennant for the New York Giants?

a. Monte Irvin
b. Willie Mays
c. Willie McCovey
d. Alvin Dark
e. Carl Erskine

**55** Which of the following teams have been in the same city for the entire history of the franchise?

a. Atlanta Braves
b. Minnesota Twins
c. Texas Rangers
d. Montréal Expos
e. Baltimore Orioles

**56** There he goes again! Who doesn't fit?

a. Lou Pinella
b. Clyde King
c. Frank Howard
d. Gene Michael
e. Billy Martin

## 57 Forgot to pack the bags. Who doesn't fit?

a. Sandy Koufax
b. Pee Wee Reese
c. Duke Snider
d. Roy Campanella
e. Junior Gilliam

## 58 Who is the only pitcher to appear in all seven games of a world series?

a. Kent Tekulve
b. Todd Worrell
c. Roger McDowell
d. Darold Knowles
e. Rollie Fingers

## 59 Who holds the record for the most saves in World Series play?

a. Tug McGraw
b. Kent Tekulve
c. Rich Gossage
d. Rollie Fingers
e. Dennis Eckersley

## 60 Rank in order of most relief wins.

a. Elroy Face
b. Lindy McDaniel
c. Hoyt Wilhelm
d. Kent Tekulve
e. Rollie Fingers

## 61 Before 1900, who holds the record for most victories in a season?

a. Hoss Radbourn
b. Cy Young
c. Guy Hecker
d. George Bradley
e. Al Maul

## 62 Born too late. Who doesn't fit?

   a. Nap Lajoie
   b. Cap Anson
   c. Honus Wagner
   d. Billy Hamilton
   e. Eddie Collins

## 63 Put the following events in the proper chronological order.

   a. "Take Me Out To the Ball Game" begins to be sung at games
   b. First year a player hits more than 10 home runs in a single season
   c. Major League attendance hits 10 million fans for a single year
   d. Babe Ruth hits his first Major League home run
   e. Ty Cobb gets his first base hit

## 64 Not in the 300 club. Who doesn't belong?

   a. Eddie Plank
   b. Early Wynn
   c. Jim Palmer
   d. Don Sutton
   e. Lefty Grove

## 65 It takes time. Who's the odd man out?

   a. Don Newcombe
   b. Joe Black
   c. Richie Allen
   d. Jerry Koosman
   e. Frank Robinson

## 66 What team went the most consecutive seasons without finishing in last place?

   a. Brooklyn/Los Angeles Dodgers
   b. New York Yankees
   c. Detroit Tigers
   d. New York/San Francisco Giants
   e. Boston Red Sox

**67** Never there in the end.  Who doesn't fit?
   a. Lindy McDaniel
   b. Ron Perranoski
   c. Sam McDowell
   d. Stu Miller
   e. Al Harbosky

# Smarter-Than-Most Answers

*(Score 1 point for each correct answer. For multiple choice, score 1 point if all are correct; 1/2 point if 3 are correct.)*

1. d. Frank Robinson did eight times.
2. b. George Brett was the American League batting champion in 1976, 1980 and 1990.
3. d. In 1901 Sam Crawford led the National League with 16 home runs while playing for the Cincinnatti Reds. Seven years later in 1908 his 7 home runs led all American league sluggers.
4. b. Lou Gehrig hit 23 grand slam home runs during his 17 year career as a New York Yankee.
5. d. Ronald Reagan played Grover Cleveland Alexander in a movie. He never played Walter Johnson.
6. 1-d, 2-b, 3-e, 4-c, 5-a
7. a. Steve Carlton struck out 4,136 batters in his 24-year career.
8. e. The Dodgers lost 12 World Series, 8 of them to the New York Yankees.
9. 1-d,  2-e,  3-b,  4-c,  5-a
10. c . At the time of his 30th birthday Phil Niekro had won only 31 games. He would go on to win 318 games before retiring in 1987 at age 48.
11. d. Bobby and Barry Bonds have hit 508 home runs through the 1992 season.
12. d. Wade Boggs had 200 or more base hits in seven consecutive seasons (1983-1989).

13. c. "The Duke of Flatbush" Duke Snider was the greatest slugger in the 1950's, slugging 326 homers during the decade while playing for the Brooklyn Dodgers.
14. a. Walter Johnson threw 110 shutouts in his career.
15. d. Grover Alexander threw sixteen shutouts in 1916 while pitching for the Philadelphia Phillies.
16. a. New York Giant pitcher Richard "Rube" Marquard won 19 consecutive games in 1912.
17. e. Jimmie Foxx hit 30 or more home runs in 12 consecutive seasons (1929-1940).
18. a. Cliff Johnson hit 20 pinch hit home runs in his 15 year career.
19. c. Ty Cobb was the only one never suspended from Major League baseball.
20. 1-c, 2-e, 3-d, 4-a, 5-b
21. e. Jimmie Wilson had a .401 winning percentage in his 9-year managerial career.
22. b. Casey Stengel
23. d. Helen Britton ran the St. Louis Cardinals from 1911 to 1916.
24. c. Babe Ruth did it 72 times in his career.
25. b. Paul Waner hit an extra-base hit in 14 consecutive games while playing for the Pittsburgh Pirates in 1927.
26. d. In 1972 Steve Carlton won 27 of his team's 59 victories, in a sense responsible for 45.6% of the Phillies success.
27. b. Christy Mathewson won 128 games in his first five seasons (1901-1905).
28. b. Grover "Pete" Alexander won 28 games in his rookie campaign.
29. c. Frankie Hayes played 312 consecutive games at catcher from October 3, 1943 to April 21, 1946 while playing for the Philadelphia A's and Cleveland Indians.
30. d. Ty Cobb stole home 54 times.
31. d. On two different occasions during the the 1912 season Eddie Collins stole 6 bases in one game.

32. d. The Baltimore Orioles began the 1988 season by losing 21 straight games.
33. c. The 1987 Minnesota Twins went 85-77 (.525) for the lowest winning percentage by a world series winning team.
34. d. The 1916 Philadelphia Athletics went 36-117 for a .235 winning percentage, the worst in major league history.
35. b. Roberto Clemente was inducted into the Hall of Fame by special election in 1973.
36. d. Cal Hubbard was elected to Canton after a career as a tackle in the NFL and then went on the become a Major League umpire, later elected to Cooperstown.
37. b. Reggie Jackson is the only one to play in a World Series game.
38. b. In 1966, St. Louis Cardinal Tim McCarver was the only catcher in National League history to lead the league.
39. a. In 1986 Don Mattingly played in all 162 games, had 677 at bats and never stole a base.
40. c. Los Angeles Dodger pitcher Al Downing threw the pitch that put Aaron in the record books.
41. c. In 1986, Bert Blyleven gave up 50 home runs in 271 2/3 innings while pitching for the Minnesota Twins.
42. b. Robin Roberts allowed 505 home runs during his career with the Philadelphia Phillies.
43. b. Rookie Phillie second baseman Mickey Morandini accomplished the feat in 1992 against the Pittsburgh Pirates.
44. d. Paul Molitor is the only player who is not a switch hitter.
45. a. Lefty Gomez had six World Series victories without ever suffering a loss.
46. c. At age 45 years, 3 months and 7 days, Jack Quinn pitched for the Philadelphia A's in the 1929 series. He had a no-decision.

47. c (1947), e (1955), a (1966), d (1972), b (1975)
48. c. Whitey Ford went 29 2/3 innings in world series play without giving up a run.
49. 1-a, 2-c, 3-d, 4-e, 5-b
50. 1-d, 2-c, 3-e, 4-a, 5-b
51. 1-e, 2-d, 3-a, 4-c, 5-b
52. 1-e, 2-a, 3-b, 4-d, 5-c
53. e. Dave Stewart has won 8 games in LCS play during his career.
54. b. Playing in his rookie season, Willie Mays sat on-deck as Bobby Thomson hit his famous home run.
55. d. The Expos have been playing in Montréal ever since they began Major League play in 1969.
56. c. Frank Howard is the only one who has never managed the Yankees. Yet.
57. d. Roy Campanella is the only one to play on just the Brooklyn Dodgers. All the others played in both Brooklyn and Los Angeles.
58. d. Oakland A's reliever Darol Knowles pitched in all seven games in the 1973 world series, earning 2 saves with an ERA of 0.00.
59. d. Rollie Fingers had six saves.
60. c (124), b (119), e (107), a (96), d (94)
61. a. In 1884, pitching for Providence, Charley "Hoss" Radbourn won 59 games.
62. e. Eddie Collins is the only player who did not play in the 19th century.
63. b-1901, e-1905, a-1908, d-1914, c-1930
64. c. Jim Palmer is the only pitcher to win less than 300 games.
65. d. Jerry Koosman is the only player not to have won the Rookie of the Year Award.
66. a. The Dodgers went 85 consecutive years without finishing in last place (1906-1991).
67. c. Sam McDowell is the only pitcher who was primarily a starter and not a reliever.

# Genius Questions

*Time limit: 60 minutes*

### 1 Who is the only pitcher to win a world series game in three different decades?

   a. Jim Palmer
   b. Whitey Ford
   c. Johnny Podres
   d. Tom Seaver
   e. Bob Welch

### 2 Who is the only player to hit a home run in his first two major league at-bats?

   a. Bert Campaneris
   b. Charlie Jamieson
   c. Bob Nieman
   d. Andy Pafko
   e. Wally Post

### 3 What pitcher was on the mound when Joe DiMaggio's 56 game hitting streak came to an end?

   a. Bob Feller
   b. Jim Bagby
   c. Al Smith
   d. Hal Newhouser
   e. Mel Harder

### 4 Who is the only pitcher to have over 3,000 strikeouts and less than 1,000 walks?

   a. Jim Bunning
   b. Bob Gibson
   c. Don Sutton
   d. Fergie Jenkins
   e. Vida Blue

## 5 Who is the only player to hit for the cycle in both leagues?

   a. Kirk Gibson
   b. Joe Carter
   c. Bob Watson
   d. Bobby Bonds
   e. Mookie Wilson

## 6 Who hit the most home runs in the 19th century?

   a. Dan Brouthers
   b. Sam Thompson
   c. Buck Ewing
   d. Roger Connor
   e. Cap Anson

## 7 What Negro League catcher threw out Ty Cobb trying to steal three times during an exhibition game?

   a. Josh Gibson
   b. Herman Bell
   c. James Jeffries
   d. Bruce Petway
   e. Poindexter Williams

## 8 Whose lifetime home run record did Babe Ruth eclipse?

   a. Frank Baker
   b. Zack Wheat
   c. Cap Anson
   d. Roger Connor
   e. Dan Brouthers

## 9  Who is the only player to get hits for two different teams in two different cities on the same day?

   a. Felix Milan
   b. Joel Youngblood
   c. Steve Henderson
   d. Doug Goldfein
   e. Rusy Staub

## 10  Rank in chronological order:

   a. Spitball is abolished.
   b. First radio announcer uses the phrase "Going, going, gone."
   c. Satchel Paige makes his professional debut.
   d. First radio broadcast of a major league game.
   e. Yankee Stadium is built.

## 11  Who were the only brothers to combine on a shut-out?

   a. Dizzy and Paul Dean
   b. Bob and Ken Forsch
   c. Rick and Paul Reuschel
   d. Stan and Harry Coveleski
   e. Phil and Joe Niekro

## 12  Rank the following brothers from most career hits to fewest:

   a. Joe, Vince and Dom DiMaggio
   b. Paul and Lloyd Waner
   c. Ken, Clete and Cloyd Boyer
   d. Hank and Tommy Aaron
   e. Felipe, Matty and Jesus Alou

## 13 Who were the first brother battery in the major leagues (after 1900)?

a. Mort and Walker Cooper
b. Jack and Mike O'Neill
c. Homer and Thommy Thompson
d. Rick and Wes Ferrel
e. Johnnny and Elmer Riddle

## 14 Who holds the record for the highest on base percentage in a single season?

a. Pete Rose
b. Rod Carew
c. Ty Cobb
d. Babe Ruth
e. Ted Williams

## 15 Who holds the record for the most walks given up by a pitcher in a season?

a. Kid Nichols
b. Bob Feller
c. Amos Rusie
d. Tim Keefe
e. Joe McGinnity

## 16 Who was the only player to turn an unassisted triple play in the world series?

a. Goose Goslin
b. Bill Wambsganss
c. Frank "Home Run" Baker
d. Dave Bancroft
e. Eddie Collins

## 17 Turning Japanese. Who doesn't belong?

a. Randy Bass
b. Dave Parker
c. Bob Horner
d. Felix Milan
e. Leron Lee

Baseball Genius Questions

## 18 What future hall of famer played with the Harlem Globetrotters?

   a. Don Newcombe
   b. Larry Doby
   c. Bob Gibson
   d. Lou Brock
   e. Maury Wills

## 19 Versatility. Odd one out?

   a. Dick Groat
   b. Ron Reed
   c. Bo Jackson
   d. Jackie Robinson
   e. Jim Thorpe

## 20 Who is the only player to be named to the All-American college basketball team and win a Major League MVP award?

   a. Dave Winfield
   b. Danny Ainge
   c. Jim Konstanty
   d. Dick Groat
   e. Michael Jordan

## 21 Who holds the Minor League record for the most career home runs?

   a. Hector Espino
   b. Merv Connors
   c. Steve Balboni
   d. Harry Strohm
   e. Pedro Hernandez

## 22 What player has gone the most consecutive games without striking out?

   a. Tommy Holmes
   b. Nellie Fox
   c. Joe Sewell
   d. Lloyd Waner
   e. Carey Selph

## 23 What pitcher holds the record for the most consecutive innings without giving up a walk?

   a. Dick Donovan
   b. Lee Stange
   c. Don Drysdale
   d. Joe Nuxhall
   e. Bill Fischer

## 24 Who holds the record for the most combined hits and walks in a season?

   a. Rickey Henderson
   b. Babe Ruth
   c. Ted Williams
   d. George Sisler
   e. Tony Gwynn

## 25 Who has the most pinch-hit homers in a season?

   a. Willie McCovey
   b. Ernie Lombardi
   c. Cliff Johnson
   d. Johnny Frederick
   e. Cy Williams

## 26 Who holds the record for most pinch-hit RBI's in a World Series?

a. Bernie Carbo
b. Dusty Rhodes
c. Johnny Mize
d. Dave Rickets
e. Andy Pafko

## 27 Successes in both leagues. Who doesn't fit?

a. Ferguson Jenkins
b. Jim Bunning
c. Jim Kaat
d. Gaylord Perry
e. Nolan Ryan

## 28 Match the pitcher with the record or feat:

1. Wes Ferrel
2. Tony Cloninger
3. Jim Tobin
4. Roric Harrison
5. Ken Brett

a. Only pitcher to 3 HR's in a game
b. Most career HRs by a pitcher
c. Most consecutive games hitting at least 1 HR as a pitcher
d. Only pitcher to hit two grand slams in a game
e. Last AL pitcher to hit a home run in a regular season game

## 29 What pitcher won 30 or more games in the most seasons?

a. Cy Young
b. Kid Nichols
c. Walter Johnson
d. Amos Rusie
e. Tim Keefe

## 30 Who is the only man to win a pennant in his lone season as manager?

a. George Wright
b. Ted Turner
c. Bill Dickey
d. Nat Hicks
e. Fred Hoey

## 31 Who holds the record for the most seasons as a player and/or manager without a world series appearance?

a. Gene Mauch
b. Ernie Banks
c. Joe Torre
d. Leo Durocher
e. Bucky Harris

## 32 What future manager hit a home run in his first Major League at-bat?

a. Danny Murtaugh
b. Del Crandall
c. Chuck Tanner
d. Chuck Cottier
e. Dick Howser

## 33 Who is the only Hall of Fame pitcher to hit a homerun in their first major league at-bat?

a. Hoyt Wilhelm
b. Lefty Gomez
c. Waite Hoyt
d. Red Faber
e. Rollie Fingers

## 34 Who is the only pitcher-manager to win a World Series (since 1900)?

- a. Walter Johnson
- b. Clark Griffith
- c. Cy Young
- d. Roger Craig
- e. John McGraw

## 35 Broad success. Who doesn't fit?

- a. Sparky Anderson
- b. Alvin Dark
- c. Joe McCarthy
- d. Earl Weaver
- e. Dick Williams

## 36 Who was the first Hall of Fame Player to later become an umpire?

- a. Dan Brouthers
- b. Tim Keefe
- c. Kid Nichols
- d. Ed Walston
- e. Brickyard Kennedy

## 37 What major league umpire served the most years?

- a. Ron Luciano
- b. Eddie Rommel
- c. Bill Klem
- d. Doug Harvey
- e. Babe Pinelli

**38** What is the legal limit for the amount of pine tar that can extend from the bat handles?

   a. 6 inches
   b. 12 inches
   c. 15 inches
   d. 18 inches
   e. 21 inches

**39** Game of inches. Match the following:

   1. Length of the front part of home plate
   2. How much higher the pitcher's mound is than home plate
   3. Legal limit for a bat
   4. Legal limit for the circumference of a catcher's mitt
   5. Legal limit for the circumference of a baseball

   a. 42 inches
   b. 17 inches
   c. 38 inches
   d. 10 inches
   e. 9 1/4 inches

**40** Match the player with his nickname:

   1. Doug Rader
   2. Duke Snider
   3. Clark Griffith
   4. Harvey Haddix
   5. Tris Speaker

   a. "The Grey Eagle"
   b. "The Old Fox"
   c. "The Red Rooster"
   d. "The Silver Fox"
   e. "The Kitten"

**41** Who is the only player to hit a ball completely out of Dodger stadium?

   a. Dave Kingman
   b. Billy Williams
   c. Bob Horner
   d. Willie Stargell
   e. Willie McCovey

52   Baseball Genius Questions

## 42 What player has gone the most at-bats in a season without hitting a triple?

a. Willie Horton
b. Ed Kranepool
c. Cookie Rojas
d. Ken Singleton
e. Ken Boyer

## 43 What player hit into the fewest double plays per at bat?

a. Dick McAuliffe
b. Dave Cash
c. Willie Wilson
d. Don Buford
e. Tommie Agee

## 44 What pitcher holds the record for most consecutive wins on a losing team?

a. Robin Roberts
b. Steve Carlton
c. Walter Johnson
d. Jerry Koosman
e. Ned Garver

## 45 Who is credited with inventing the curveball?

a. Al Spalding
b. Elmer Stricklett
c. Candy Cummings
d. Cap Anson
e. George Bradley

## 46 Who got the first ever National League base hit ?

- a. Jim O'Rourke
- b. Ross Barnes
- c. Cap Anson
- d. Jack Burdock
- e. Lip Pike

## 47 Who hit the first home run in the American League?

- a. Ollie Pickering
- b. Nap Lajoie
- c. Erv Beck
- d. Buck Freeman
- e. Mike Grady

## 48 What pitcher went the most consecutive innings without giving up a home run?

- a. Terry Forster
- b. Tim Burke
- c. Ron Perranoski
- d. Greg Minton
- e. Lynn McGlothen

## 49 What catcher holds the record for the most no-hitters caught?

- a. Ray Schalk
- b. Johnny Roseboro
- c. Johnny Kling
- d. Yogi Berra
- e. Gene Tenace

## 50 What first baseman holds the record for the most assists in a season?

a. Gil Hodges
b. George Scott
c. Bill Buckner
d. Keith Hernandez
e. Steve Garvey

## 51 What shortstop-2nd base combination holds the record for the most double plays in a season?

a. Dave Cash-Larry Bowa (Philadelphia Phillies)
b. Joe Tinker-Johnny Evers (Chicago Cubs)
c. Luis Aparicio-Nellie Fox (Chicago White Sox)
d. Gene Alley-Bill Mazeroski (Pittsburgh Pirates)
e. Phil Rizzuto-Joe Gordon (New York Yankees)

## 52 What regular holds the record for the lowest single-season fielding average since 1901?

a. Neal Ball
b. Bill Keister
c. Dick Allen
d. Heine Zimmerman
e. Charlie Pick

## 53 Who was the announcer for the first radio broadcast?

a. Tommy Cowan
b. Mel Allen
c. Harold Arlen
d. Jack Graney
e. Graham MacNamee

## 54 Who was the last National League manager to win three consecutive pennants?

a. Walter Alston
b. John McGraw
c. Danny Murtaugh
d. Sparky Anderson
e. Billy Southworth

## 55 Who was the first major-leaguer drafted for World War II?

a. Hank Greenberg
b. Dom DiMaggio
c. Hugh Mulcahy
d. Buddy Kerr
e. Joe Heving

## 56 Which came first? Rank in chronological order:

a. Four balls and three strikes become the rule
b. 20,000 fans attend a game
c. First U.S. president attends a game
d. The balk rule is implemented
e. American League begins

## 57 What player played on the most teams for at least one full season?

a. Bobo Newsom
b. Gaylord Perry
c. Alex Johnson
d. Dave Henderson
e. Tommy Davis

**58** Who is the only member of the Braves organization to play in Boston, Milwaukee and Atlanta?

   a. Warren Spahn
   b. Hank Aaron
   c. Joe Adcock
   d. Eddie Mathews
   e. Johnny Sain

**59** What pitcher at age 40 or older holds the record for the most wins in a season?

   a. Warren Spahn
   b. Satchel Paige
   c. Nolan Ryan
   d. Phil Niekro
   e. Gaylord Perry

**60** Rank in order age in which they played their last major league game (from oldest to youngest):

   a. Tommy John
   b. Satchel Paige
   c. Warren Spahn
   d. Phil Niekro
   e. Gaylord Perry

**61** What pitching duo combined for the most strike-outs in a season?

   a. Nolan Ryan and Bill Singer (1973)
   b. Tom Seaver and Jerry Koosman (1972)
   c. Don Drysdale and Sandy Koufax (1965)
   d. Dwight Gooden and Sid Fernandez (1985)
   e. Warren Spahn and Lew Burdette (1958)

**62** What pitching staff holds the record for the lowest team ERA in a world series?
   a. 1966 Baltimore Orioles
   b. 1974 Oakland Athletics
   c. 1938 New York Yankees
   d. 1905 New York Giants
   e. 1907 Chicago Cubs

**63** Which pitcher holds the lifetime record for the lowest opponent's batting average?
   a. J.R. Richard
   b. Sandy Koufax
   c. Walter Johnson
   d. Nolan Ryan
   e. Bob Feller

**64** Who holds the single-season record for most strike-outs per nine innings?
   a. Sandy Koufax
   b. Nolan Ryan
   c. J.R. Richard
   d. Roger Clemens
   e. Dwight Gooden

**65** Which short stop since 1900 had the best batting average in a single season?
   a. Honus Wagner
   b. Rabbit Maranville
   c. Hughie Jennings
   d. Luke Appling
   e. Joe Cronin

## 66 What pitcher holds the record for the most career relief losses?

  a. Kent Tekulve
  b. Bruce Sutter
  c. Sparky Lyle
  d. Gene Garber
  e. Hoyt Wilhem

# *Genius* Answers

*(Score 1 point for each correct answer. For multiple choice score 1 point if all are correct; 1/2 point if 3 are correct).*

1. a. Baltimore Oriole Jim Palmer won games in the 1966, 1970, 1971 and 1983 World Series.
2. c. St. Louis Brown Bob Nieman hit two homeruns in his first two at-bats in 1951.
3. b. Jim Bagby of the Cleveland Indians was the pitcher who ended Joe DiMaggio's chance of extending his streak.
4. d. Fergie Jenkins is 9th on the all-time strike-out list with 3,192, but with 997 lifetime walks, is the only pitcher in the 3,000 club to have less than 1,000 walks.
5. c. Bob Watson hit for the cycle while playing for the Houston Astros in 1977 and then in 1979 as a Boston Red Sox.
6. d. Roger Connor hit 138 home runs from 1880 to 1897.
7. d. Bruce Petway
8. d. Roger Connor held the lifetime HR record with 138 HR's before it was surpassed by Babe Ruth in 1921.
9. b. In the 1982 season Joel Youngblood accomplished the feat of getting a base hit on two different teams on the same day. He began the day as a Met and got a hit in a day game. That same day he was traded to Montréal and proceeded to get a hit in a night game.

10. a(1920), b(1921), e(1923), c(1926), b(1929)
11. c. Chicago Cub pitchers Rick and Paul Reuschel combined for a 7-0 shutout against the Los Angeles Dodgers in 1975.
12. b (5,611), a (5,553), e (5,094), d (3,987), c (3,559)
13. b. Catcher Jack and Pitcher Mike O'Neill played together for the 1902 St. Louis Cardinals.
14. e. Ted Williams had a .551 OBP in 1941 for the Boston Red Sox.
15. c. Amos Rusie gave a free ride to 289 batters in the 1890 season.
16. b. With Brooklyn Dodger Clarence Mitchel at-bat, Cleveland Indian second baseman Bill Wambsganss completed an unassisted triple play in the 1920 world series.
17. b. Dave Parker is the only player never to play professional baseball in Japan.
18. c. Bob Gibson, before beginning his Major League baseball career with the St. Louis Cardinals
19. d. Jackie Robinson is the only player not to have played two professional sports.
20. d. Dick Groat was an All-American while playing for the Duke Blue Devils and later went on to win the National League MVP in 1960.
21. a. Hector Espino hit 484 home runs in the minor leagues. He never hit a home run in the majors.
22. b. In 1958 Nellie Fox went 98 games without striking out.
23. e. In 1962, Kansas City A's pitcher Bill Fischer went 82 2/3 innings without giving up a walk.
24. b. Babe Ruth had 205 hits and 170 walks in 1923 for a record setting combination of .375.
25. d. Johnny Frederick hit 6 pinch-hit homers for the Brooklyn Dodgers in 1932.
26. b. Dusty Rhodes had 6 RBI's as a pinch hitter for the New York Giants in the 1954 season.
27. c. Jim Kaat is the only pitcher not to win 100 games in each league.

<u>Baseball Genius Answers</u>

28. 1-b, 2-d, 3-a, 4-e, 5-c
29. b. Kid Nichols did it seven times (1891-1894, 1896-1898).
30. a. George Wright won the pennant as the providence manager in 1879.
31. a. Gene Mauch has gone 35 years in the Major League (9 years as a player and 26 years as a manager) without ever going to the World Series.
32. c. Chuck Tanner hit a home run on his first pitch in 1955 as a Milwaukee Brewer.
33. a. New York Giant pitcher Hoyt Wilhelm hit a home run in his first at-bat in 1952. He never hit a home run again.
34. b. Clark Griffith led the Chicago White Sox to the American League pennant in 1901.
35. d. Earl Weaver is the only manager never to have taken a team from each league to the world series.
36. b. Tim Keefe, a pitcher from 1880-1893, was also an umpire elected to the Hall of Fame in 1964.
37. c. Bill Klem was an umpire for a record setting 37 years.
38. d. As established in 1976, any material including pine tar cannot extend past the 18 inch limitation from the handle of the bat.
39. 1-b, 2-d, 3-a, 4-c, 5-e
40. 1-c, 2-d, 3-b, 4-e, 5-a
41. d. Willie Stargell did it twice.
42. c. In 1968 Philadelphia Phillie Cookie Rojas had 621 at-bats without hitting a triple.
43. d. Don Buford holds the record for fewest double per at-bat grounding into a double play once in every 138 times at bat.
44. b. Steve Carlton won 15 consecutive games for the last place Phillies in 1972.
45. c. Though no one is certain, Candy Cummings is often credited with inventing the curveball sometime during the 1860's.

46. a. Boston's Jim O'Rourke singled in the top of the first inning in the first National League game.
47. c. Erv Beck of the Cleveland Indians hit the first home run in American League play.
48. d. Greg Minton went 269 2/3 innings (over 4 seasons) without allowing a home run.
49. a. Ray Schalk caught 4 no-hit games during 18 year career.
50. c. In 1984 Bill Buckner had 189 assists, but will always be remembered for the one play he did not make.
51. d. The Pittsburgh Pirate 2B-SS combo of Bill Mazeroski and Gene Alley had 289 double plays in 1966.
52. b. In 1901 Baltimore Oriole short stop Bill Keister fielded .851 and made 97 errors.
53. c. In 1921 Harold Arlen of KDKA radio in Pittsburgh was the voice for the first major league broadcast as the Pirates defeated the Phillies 8-5.
54. e. Billy Southworth led the St. Louis Cardinals to three straight pennants from 1942-1944.
55. c. On March 8, 1941, Philadelphia Phillie pitcher Mulcahy became the first player drafted in preparation for World War II.
56. b (1886), a (1889), c (1892), d (1898), e (1901)
57. c. Alex Johnson played a full season on 8 different teams.
58. d. Eddie Mathews began his career as a Boston Brave in 1952 and made the move with the Braves to Milwaukee in 1953 and then to Atlanta in 1966.
59. a. At age 43, Warren Spahn won 23 games for the Milwaukee Braves.
60. b (59 years old), d(48), a(46), e(45), c(44)
61. a. In 1973 Nolan Ryan struck out 383 batters and Bill Singer 241 for a record setting 624 batters while pitching for the California Angels.

62. d. The 1905 New York Giant pitching staff had a 0.00 Team ERA en route to a 5 game victory over the Philadelphia A's.
63. d. Batters who faced Nolan Ryan (through the 1992 season) hit .203.
64. b. At age 40, Nolan Ryan struck out an average of 11.48 batters per game during the 1987 season.
65. d. Luke Appling hit .388 in 1936 for the Chicago White Sox.
66. d. Gene Garber lost 108 games in relief.